intelligence would develop fully and automatically in a secure and ha_____ *but this is not necessarily so.* Rest_____s too restrained by a_____s, can also 'tidy up' _____s potential of intellig_____g him or her dull and already inhibited at an early age.

The first two years are very important. If a child's potential intelligence has been expanded fully by stimulating toys, activities and conversation, then the third year should be one of even more rapidly expanding physical and mental activity.

Maybe there are plenty of toys in the home, but do these contribute to your child's development? Has he handled objects big and small, soft and hard? Does he know the feel of grass, stones or leaves, tinfoil or tissue paper? Do let him find out that water will do what he wishes, that he can so masterfully fill and empty

things, that sand can be poured, pushed and pressed and stay that way, and that he can use it to hide things in and discover them again.

Cartons and boxes will stack and build like bricks; plastic bottles can be cut or shaped for water or sand play or as fitting toys – all giving good opportunities for helping your child's development, once you realise the significance of these materials to him. *The subsequent purchase of a really worth-while toy is then the more easily afforded.*

By the age of two, your child may have an established interest in picture and story books which have been read to him and talked about with him. Many Ladybird books are ideal for this purpose, especially those included in the Ladybird 'Under Five' series and those recommended on page 28 of this book.

Your child's vocabulary, so vital to mental and emotional development, will be growing rapidly during his third year. It will, however, depend largely on the attitude of grown-ups – who should always be ready to talk on all topics likely to interest, educate or amuse him. This book is intended to help and stimulate all parents who realise the importance of using to the full those situations and materials most likely to help develop their child's potential for learning.

Freed

BOOK 2
Two to three years

THE LADYBIRD 'UNDER FIVE' SERIES

Learning
with
Mother

by ETHEL and HARRY WINGFIELD

Publishers: Ladybird Books Ltd . Loughborough
© Ladybird Books Ltd (formerly Wills & Hepworth Ltd) 1970
Printed in England

Water

Water is one of the joys of childhood, and the most satisfying of all play material. It is also the cheapest! The child's sense of hearing, sight and touch are used and excited by it. Watch him on the beach, playing in the shallow sea, tossing it high so that it falls over him in a shower. He will use all his energy beating it into a foam, he feels it thrusting against his legs or lapping gently over his toes. He is exhilarated by the never-ending movement in which he can become so completely involved. He can use his whole body with which to make a tremendous splash, plop pebbles into the oncoming waves, or trickle the water from bucket to bucket. With it he can wash the sand from buckets, seaweed and shells, as well as from between his toes. Small wonder that a child is left content, relaxed and happy after play with water.

Talk to your child about the picture, about the sound and feel of the water, the colour of the buckets, about his or her visit to the seaside and the paddling pool, and what was done there.

Of course, there can be water-play at home, too . . .

7214 0257 7

Water-play at home

Plastic curtaining material, elastic and tape will make a waterproof apron and cuffs (which will last many months). If the apron overlaps the wellingtons, so much the better. For water-play, you can make holes in a plastic container. Children love blowing bubbles into water through a piece of plastic tubing. The tubing can also be used to join two plastic bottles together, as illustrated. The child can watch the bottles filling and emptying, according to which is held the higher – particularly if the tube and bottles are clear plastic and the water tinted with edible colouring. Your old kettle or metal teapot will also be greatly appreciated. Of course, the water should be warmed. Indoors, perhaps in the kitchen, a small amount of water is equally satisfactory.

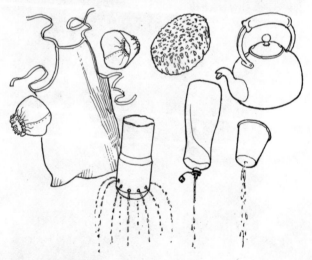

Talk about the picture.

Sand

Sand can be built up, knocked down, dug into or (gently) scattered, patted into shapes or just trickled through fingers or toes. Here is play material over which a child is complete master!

Talk to your child about the picture. For example, the boy is using a lollipop stick to draw in the sand. The girl has made a flag from a toffee paper and a lollipop stick. Have they found any seaweed or shells?

8

Sand-play at home

Four lengths of planed wood and four corner pieces, screwed together as illustrated, will make a sand-frame to stand on a flat surface.

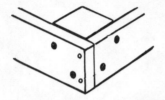 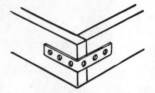

SILVER SAND is best, and may be bought from a hardware store or seed merchant. Alternatively, put the sand in a hole with concrete slabs around to facilitate sweeping back. For moulding shapes, the sand will need to be damp, of course. Rolled flat, it makes a firm surface on which to press patterns of hands, lids or anything which makes an interesting impression. Even a bowl or box of sand is better than none at all.

Include a small broom : sweeping the sand back where it belongs is part of the fun. Do not forget a wire mesh cover to keep away animals when the sand is not being used. Children play safely and constructively for long periods with sand, so a sand-pit is well worth providing.

Ask your child to name the objects in the picture – what the girl is holding, what the boy is holding – and so on. Ask him how many brooms or spades there are, and how many children.

Dry sand

Silver sand, when dry, behaves almost like a liquid. Let it run through an old colander, funnel, sink-tidy or our plastic-bottle-with-holes. It moves fast, fills and empties as quickly as water, and what an exciting noise it makes spattering down onto paper!

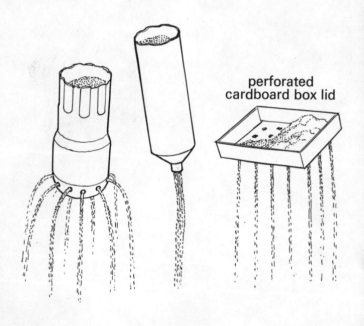

perforated
cardboard box lid

Talk about the picture. Point out the sink-tidy, the strainer, the colander, the sand running down onto the newspaper etc.

Shells and pebbles

Children delight in handling shells and pebbles, exploring their shapes and textures, sorting and emptying them from one container to another, forming them into patterns or rattling them in tins. Use them for counting – "one cockle shell, two winkle shells, three limpet shells" – and so on.* Children learn eagerly and easily about objects they can see and handle for themselves. Shells can often be bought from toy shops.

Talk about the picture. Mother has lent the children her cake tin for sorting shells. There are long shells, white shells, yellow shells, round shells – all kinds of shells! She has cut out some big numbers from newspaper for the children to cover with shells!

*See the Ladybird Book of the Seashore and Seashore Life

Parks and adventure playgrounds

These offer the very young child the opportunity to watch and to mix with other children. With mother's help, he can use the small slide and swing and, in the company of others, try himself out on the climbing frame. He will learn that he has nothing to fear from other children, and this is an important step forward in his social development.

Talk about the children in the picture and what they are doing. If your child has been to a playground, he will want to tell you what he did there.

A playground in the garden

This is easily made with one or two strong wooden boxes, a length of timber, cartons and packing cases, all carefully looked over for sharp edges, nails and splinters.

Let your child learn for himself what he can and cannot do. From this freedom he will develop mental as well as physical stability and confidence, and will also learn to be cautious.

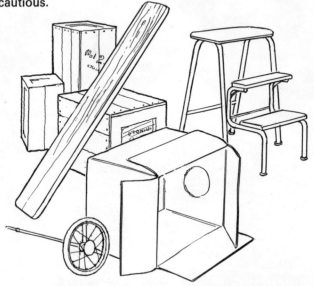

Talk about the children peeping, balancing and crawling. Ask what the child with the wheel might be doing. If your child has no playmates, you must be prepared to be a passenger in a make-believe bus! Save your old tickets for this.

Doing what Mother or Father does

Doing what they see Mother or Father do is all-important to children at this age and should be encouraged. Children have a need for identification with the adult world around them and this sort of play provides satisfaction and reassurance.

The pegs illustrated have been painted in four different colours to match the painted sides of the biscuit tin, or coloured spring-pegs would do. You then have a colour-matching and counting toy. Pegging-out clothes is not so very easy for the two year old, but a whole row of washing, hung out, the result of much persistent effort, really pleases. Your praise and encouragement is necessary, as always.

Talk about the picture – what the children are doing, what garments are on the line, the colours of clothes, bowls and pegs, whether it is a good day for drying – and why.

Insects

Children are fascinated by insects and other small creatures. If Mother shows interest also, and not revulsion, a good atmosphere is created for teaching the child simple facts about living things with which they come into contact.

Parents and children can learn together from the many attractive and factual Ladybird books now available, and so establish the habit of "finding out" at the precise moment when the child's interest and pleasure is aroused. Young children have insatiable curiosity about where a creature lives and sleeps, what its bed or its Mummy looks like, what it eats for dinner and whether it walks, crawls or flies. This is a healthy, normal interest and needs to be encouraged.

Little boys have two legs,
Little dogs have four,
But little furry caterpillars
Have more and more and more.

Talk about the picture.

22

Playdough   To make a clean, non-sticky play-dough which stays pliable for days (if wrapped in polythene), you will need one tablespoonful of salt to each cup of flour. Mix with water to a stiff dough. A little edible colouring adds to the appearance.

salt

flour

then

water

and mix

Talk about the picture. When making the dough, talk about the flour being smooth and soft, and the salt rough to the touch.

Playdough

This dough is play material which children love to handle. They can pinch, pull, poke and roll it, feel its shape and texture – and it provides useful exercise for small fingers. They can use, as tools, such things as blunt knives, pastry cutters, lids, matchsticks, buttons, lollipop sticks or other small articles – anything to extend the scope of their play.

Bear in mind that, at this age, the pleasure is in the mere handling of material which changes shape so easily under the warmth and pressure of small hands. Children of two years are more interested in the material as such than in aiming at results. Pummelling a large lump of dough can be an outlet for that repressed feeling, normal in a child who has had to conform for some hours, perhaps, to adult standards of behaviour.

Talk to your child about the picture – and the animal figures the children's mother has made. Why not make one yourself?

Books   Do not stack books away. Place them where their full covers can be seen. By reading aloud to your child, you are enriching his experience of speech, stimulating his own efforts at self-expression. At this age he can understand more words than he can actually say, and by listening to you he is learning to organise his own thinking. The intimate and enjoyable experience of sitting on Mother's knee at least once a day, while she reads, promises him a happy future association with books.

Here is a list of some of the Ladybird books which your child will enjoy. They are obtainable at any bookshop and most newsagents.

A Ladybird First Picture Book
A Ladybird Second Picture Book
The Farm
Numbers
The Zoo
a.b.c.
Shopping with Mother
The Party
Puppies and Kittens
Helping at Home
Play with us
A First Book of Nursery Rhymes
A Second Book of Nursery Rhymes
The Gingerbread Boy
Three Little Pigs

Talk about the picture, and encourage your child to talk about any books he or she has.

Action Rhymes

Action rhymes such as this help children to follow commands and orders and to establish memory patterns.

I'm a little teapot, short and stout,
Here's my handle, here's my spout.
When I'm ready, then I shout,
Tip me up and pour me out.

Talk about the picture and have fun doing the actions.

Toys to educate

Some toys are designed to help establish a skill or to stimulate constructive thought and imagination. The posting-box gives practice in discrimination between shapes, soon to be very important to the two year old as he begins to identify alphabet letters and numbers. The 'jumbling jumbos', typical of the strong, simply designed toys which become such great favourites, need coordination of hand and eye in order to balance them one upon another. They can also be threaded on a shoe-lace. This is a Paul and Marjorie Abbatt toy.

Posting-boxes are readily available at most toy shops.

Talk about the picture, what the children are trying to do and the various colours.

At the shops   Children get satisfaction from using the same things that Mother uses, and doing what Mother does. When out and about, shopping or in the car or bus, encourage the recognition of objects by naming and talking about them. Prompt your child to simple counting of coins or objects.

Take every opportunity to observe situations not previously noticed or talked about, so that the child returns home with his mind a little more enriched and stimulated. You, as Mother, will be encouraging your child's ability to learn. This ability must be established before a child reaches school age.

Talk about what is in the picture – what the fruit is, its colour, how many oranges the assistant holds. Ask if there are any bananas in the picture. Point out that the little girl's basket is smaller than her mother's.

Fruit peeling   Simple activities like peeling fruit can provide fun and interesting conversation. A little work with a penknife, and Mother (or Father) can transform a simple orange into any one of many amusing shapes or figures before it is finally eaten. Children enjoy the sensory experience of smell and touch. If you also have a banana or pineapple, children can play a game by closing their eyes and saying which fruit is which by its smell or its texture.

Jumbo

Little Tea-pot
back view

Cock-a-doodle

Talk about the picture. Ask what the objects shown above might be.

Painting

Kitchen paper, wallpaper or newspaper are ideal for painting on. Use children's non-toxic powder paint, mixed with water and a little flour to a creamy thickness. Let your child paint with his fingers. If brushes are used they should be sufficiently thick to make satisfying daubs of colour – or a small piece of plastic sponge is a good alternative. A tin tray or some formica can be spread with paint, and wiggles and whirls made with fingers. One colour, or perhaps two, is all a child needs at this age.

The child's pleasure and concentration will be sufficient reward for the use you allow him of the kitchen floor – or formica top. Encourage him to clear everything away afterwards, but allow plenty of time in which to do so. There will be the floor to be mopped, brushes and hands to be washed, his pictures to be hung outside to dry or left flat under the kitchen table. This is good, sound training but also, to a child, an enjoyable part of the play.

Too much mess, of course, will need some help from Mother or the child is discouraged. Be sure to save the paintings for Father to admire when he comes home.

Talk about the picture. Ask if the children are still painting or clearing-up, and what they will mop-up the floor with.

Large wooden bricks

To a child, large wooden bricks can represent many things – houses, buses, roads, garages – and are the basis of so much constructive and imaginative play. They can be simply and cheaply made.

A length of ready-planed softwood, 4"×4" or thereabouts, from your local wood merchant or hardware store, will do. Off-cuts are a good bargain. Saw off the sections accurately and sandpaper the edges and corners. It is a good idea also to have half-sizes; the child can then learn naturally – and in his own time – that two *small* bricks can take up the same space as one *large* one. Also make available cylinders and pyramids, if possible.

Talk about the picture. Count the boy's bricks. Say which child has the highest tower of bricks.

Newspaper

Children love to tear up news-paper — it makes an exciting sound and helps to get rid of a few repressions at the same time.

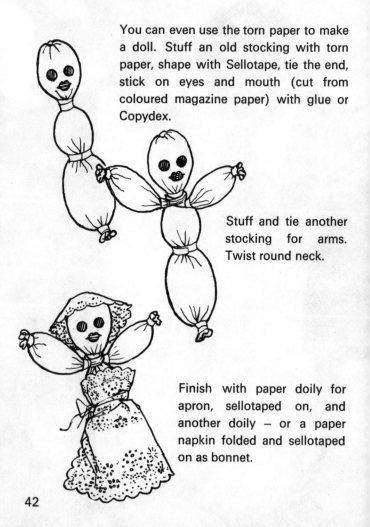

You can even use the torn paper to make a doll. Stuff an old stocking with torn paper, shape with Sellotape, tie the end, stick on eyes and mouth (cut from coloured magazine paper) with glue or Copydex.

Stuff and tie another stocking for arms. Twist round neck.

Finish with paper doily for apron, sellotaped on, and another doily — or a paper napkin folded and sellotaped on as bonnet.

Dressing-up Even two-year-olds enjoy dressing-up, especially in adult clothes. At this age it need not be part of a game, but is satisfying in itself and a source of fun.

Clothes for dressing-up can be stored in an old suitcase which children can happily rummage through. Take part in the fun and be sure to provide a mirror nearby.

Here are some articles which appeal :

Girls	Boys
Dresses	Boots
Shoes	Football gear
Feathers	Uniforms
Hats	Hats
Gloves	Caps
Pieces of fur	Socks
Old swim suits	Spectacles (without lenses)
Lipstick	Overalls
Handbags	
Scarves	

Talk about the picture. Ask which clothes are Mother's and which are Father's. Has the girl got a handbag ? Is the boy wearing a scarf ?

The Playhouse

An elaborate (and expensive) Wendy house is not really necessary. A simple arrangement, inside which the child can improvise and pretend, is quite sufficient.

Do not forget that when a child is playing indoors, all fires should be guarded.

Talk about the picture. Ask what the girl is doing and what she might be saying over the toy telephone. Is her dolly in bed?

Going to the hairdresser

Events such as a visit to the hairdresser can help to encourage self-confidence. If visiting the hairdresser is an ordeal for a child, conversation and play beforehand will help to dispel fears.

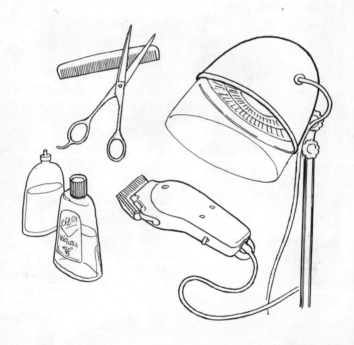

Talk about the picture, about the things the hairdresser uses, why the child has a sheet around his shoulders, and what a nice smell there is in the hairdresser's shop.

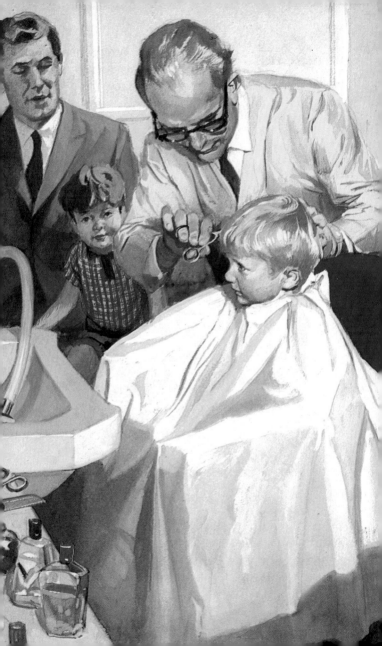

Haircuts   Here is an easy introduction to the subject – cartons filled with soil and sown with grass seed which will sprout within a fortnight and grow quite quickly, providing many successive 'haircuts' for 'Bill', 'Joe', 'Betty'.

A two-year-old is not too young to use blunt-nosed scissors.

Talk about the picture. How many little carton people have had their hair cut? How many have not?

Ask your child t
which each pictu
about what is ha
Ideas for further
in the Ladybird Pl
back cover.

also by Myra Cohn Livingston

COME AWAY *(A Margaret K. McElderry Book)*

HAPPY BIRTHDAY!

I'M HIDING

I TALK TO ELEPHANTS!

THE MALIBU
and Other Poems *(A Margaret K. McElderry Book)*

THE MOON AND A STAR
and Other Poems

WHISPERS
and Other Poems

WIDE AWAKE
and Other Poems

edited by Myra Cohn Livingston

LISTEN, CHILDREN, LISTEN:
Poems for the Very Young

SPEAK ROUGHLY TO YOUR LITTLE BOY:
A Collection of Parodies and Burlesques,
Together with the Original Poems,
Chosen and Annotated for Young People

A TUNE BEYOND US:
A Collection of Poems

WHAT A WONDERFUL BIRD THE FROG ARE:
An Assortment of Humorous Poetry and Verse

for adults

WHEN YOU ARE ALONE/IT KEEPS YOU CAPONE:
An Approach to Creative Writing with Children

THE WAY THINGS ARE AND OTHER POEMS

Myra Livingston's poetry reflects her far-ranging interests in people, in our contemporary man-made world, in the timeless verity and beauty of nature, and in amusing inconsequential detail as well as important fact. Her poetry also reflects her clear understanding and her close observation of young people as they react to the world around them— with questions, with doubts, with joyousness. The title poem sums up her feeling—and that of many of her readers: "It's today,/This road,/This knowing the road is there./A few brambles,/A few tangles,/A few scratches,/A rough stone against your toe,/But still, you've got to go/And take it./Fast, sometimes,/Or slow,/But go—/everywhere,/anywhere,/You need/to go."

Widely known as a poet, anthologist, lecturer, and as the author of a wise and practical book for adults working with children, *When You Are Alone/It Keeps You Capone: An Approach to Creative Writing With Children,* Mrs. Livingston, in this collection, offers fresh insights and special pleasures to young readers.

10 up; 5 up

THE WAY THINGS ARE AND OTHER POEMS

Myra Cohn Livingston

ILLUSTRATED BY *Jenni Oliver*

A Margaret K. McElderry Book

Atheneum 1974 New York

To Mother, again.

Text Copyright © 1974 by Myra Cohn Livingston
Illustrations Copyright © 1974 by Atheneum Publishers
All rights reserved
Library of Congress catalog card number 74-76275
ISBN 0-689-50008-4
Published simultaneously in Canada by
McClelland & Stewart, Ltd.
Manufactured in the United States of America
Printed by The Murray Printing Company
Forge Village, Massachusetts
Bound by H. Wolff, New York
Designed by Harriett Barton
First Edition

The Way Things Are

1809248

THE WAY
THINGS
ARE AND
OTHER
POEMS

It's today,
  This road,
  This knowing the road is there.
  A few brambles,
   A few tangles,
  A few scratches,
  A rough stone against your toe,
  But still, you've got to go
  And take it.
  Fast, sometimes,
  Or slow,
  But go—
               everywhere.
               anywhere
               You need
               to go.

O, I have been walking
with a bag of potato chips,
me and potato chips
munching along,

walking alone
eating potato chips,
big old potato chips,
crunching along,

walking along
munching potato chips,
me and potato chips
lunching along.

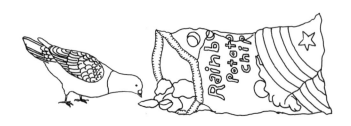

Car,
    I give you over to
    the broad flapping fingers of a
    mechanical genie,
    squeezing soap on your head,
    wooshing wax in your eyes,
    blowing air on your sides,
    brushing your bottom,
    guiding you through a white house
    and out again, on roaring tracks,
    to a little man in orange,
    wiping off your face.

Car,
    what a surprise!
    how good to see you again
    shining, gleaming.

We could be friends
Like friends are supposed to be.
You, picking up the telephone
Calling me

      to come over and play
      or take a walk,
      finding a place
      to sit and talk,

Or just goof around
Like friends do,
Me, picking up the telephone
Calling you.

Poor song,
    going around in your cassette
    over and over again, repeating
    the same old tune,
    can you breathe in there?

Come, song,
    going around in your cassette
    over and over again, break out!
    Let me play you
    fresh on my guitar!

So small a thing
This mummy lies,
Closed in death
Red-lidded eyes,
While, underneath
The swaddled clothes,
Brown arms, brown legs
Lie tight enclosed.
What miracle
If he could tell
Of other years
He knew so well;
What wonderment
To speak to me
The riddle of
His history.

It's neat, moon,
The way you stick up in that sky
And start so thin,

The way that
Every night you keep on growing,
And turn your face

Down on me
So I can see your eyes and nose
And your big mouth,

And how you
Change from silver to gold to orange
All by yourself.

It's neat, moon.
How do you do it?

The Right Place

Shoes and socks and underwear,
Books and batteries,
Games and cards and nails,
Fritos,
Hershey bars,
Mad magazines,
Scotch tape,
Baseball cards,

And whatever you need in a hurry
  is much better to keep
  where you can find it,

  under the bed.

Yesterday it was great,
A yellow day. It made my feet run
And my arms flap
And my voice sing

    (Oh sing aloud
    If sing you can!)

And I was alive.
Really alive.

Other things have happened today
And

    (Oh sing aloud
    If sing you can!)

I cannot sing.

What comes into my head
Is nothing but knowing
That it is gray
Today
And I am sad.

Gray squirrel, standing in the road,
Watch out! I've seen your kind before,
Sliding down a pine, beady eye
Focused to the other side.
I spot you as I ride,
Knowing that, when you die,
Hit by a speeding car,
Your store of nuts will not be far
Away. Listen to me. Stay
Close to the tree.
I would not kill you.
Fill your cheeks full.
Live long,
And may your winter
Be bountiful.

Lonesome all alone
Listens for the phone.

Listens for a call,
Anyone at all.

Listens for a ring,
Saying anything.

Lonesome all alone
Listens for the phone.

It's tough being short.

Of course your father tells you not to worry,
But everyone else is giant, and you're just the way
you were.
And this stupid guy says, "Hey, shorty, where'd you
get the long pants?"
Or some smart beanpole asks how it feels to be so
close to the ants?
And the school nurse says to tell her again how tall
you are, when you've already told her.
Oh, my mother says there's really no hurry
And I'll grow soon enough.

But it's tough being short.

(I wonder if Napoleon got the same old stuff?)

It beats me. The way
They sit there talking
Day after day.

Mrs. Lotts was married twice.
Her first husband lives in Sioux City.
Remember John Coleman?
He doesn't have a nickel.
My, your new dress looks nice!
That young Hodges girl is pretty.
Ruth gave me a recipe for a new kind of pickle.

(And heaven knows what all—)
Irma got sick. The Johnstones moved away.
Teddy is coming to visit. Lucille put new carpet in
    her hall.
Louise called the doctor three times yesterday.

It beats me. The way
They sit there talking
Day after day.

Arms folded, ankles crossed,
Talking and talking and talking and talking and
    talking.

Floating, floating weightless
In the nothingness of pool,
I am all wet thoughts.

Water-soaked, whirling hair
Melts into my skin.
I am bathed in blue.

Nothing beneath to feel.
Nothing but sky overhead.
I live outside myself.

I am lonesome without you seeing me.
I have grown taller.
Do you remember when
I was little and smaller?

Do you remember the time
We walked on the beach
And the big umbrella
I couldn't reach?

I can reach it now, to the top.
The sun is so hot
We stay underneath
In the coolest spot.

I have to stop writing now.
I have to go. You see
I am writing because
I am lonesome without you seeing me.

People were so small, so small.
There is an Egyptian mummy in the museum;
her face is brown; her teeth are
hanging from her mouth; she is swaddled
like a baby. She is no bigger than
a child of ten.

There is a skeleton in the museum.
Her white bones lie in a black case.
Part of her is gone. She was a
California Indian woman. She is no bigger than
a child of ten.

There is a room of French furniture in the museum.
The chairs are narrow and they stand close
To the ground. It would take a child of
ten to fit into those chairs.

And I am ten.

To try to say it,
To put it into words,
To make it come out of my mouth
  happens slowly.

There

I have said it.
Only one small say,
But it is said.

You mean, if I'd keep my room clean
And never stuff things under the bed
And hang up my jacket
And get straight *A*'s
And be polite
And work hard
And never get into trouble
I could someday grow up to be President?

Forget it!

Names

A name like Egbert, that's a blast.
Or Hepzibah. It's in the past.
I heard of a creep named Cuthbert Bede.

There's the weirdest names you sit and read—
Like Ebenezer, or Dapper Dan,
Or Abu ben Adam, or Kubla Khan,
And could you believe, could you really think
There was *really* an Engelbert Humperdinck?

Close in, near to the sand
Waves come, white and rolling.

Farther out, they turn green
With kelp snaking around the top.

But way beyond, when you squint, you can see
Hundreds of yellow sunshine spitballs.

It rattles my windows,
   spills books to the floor,
   trembles the lampshade,
   turns the floor to a bunch of waves
   and my bed to a kayak.

It makes me wonder
   where I can go
   and be unafraid.

What we need
   is a hideout near the wall
   behind the poplars, so the other guys
   won't get wise, won't spot us; just crawl
   along with me; there's a clump
   of bushes the right size.

    That's all,
        brother.
           JUMP!

           We're home free!

You find out a lot about friends,
Like if they're really friends at all.
I mean, I loan this friend a ball
And he loses it.

Boy!

Does he even say he's sorry,
Or will buy me another one?
Oh sure, he mumbles a word or two
About not having any money.

But yesterday
I saw him buying a rocky-road cone
And a bag of potato chips,
And today he was eating half a pizza.

You call *that* a friend?

I am dancing in the water,
   dancing, the white foam
   up to my ankles, dancing
   white to my knees,
   dancing, and turning back to the sand,
   around again and back,
   to my ankles, my knees and over my thighs
   and up, foam,
   dancing up to the end of my hair.

And I'm thinking how to get out
Of this stuffy room
With its big blackboards.

And I'm trying not to listen
In this boring room
To the way things *were*.

And I'm thinking about later,
Running from the room
Back into the world,

And what the guys will say when
I'm up to bat and hit
A big fat home run.

Worlds and words
Are calling me
In a book I know.

What I've never seen,
What I've never known
Comes true.

It is in my dream,
It is what I own,
It's new.

What I've never heard,
What may never be
Can be so.

I heard of poor.
It means hungry, no food,
No shoes, no place to live.
Nothing good.

It means winter nights
And being cold.
It is lonely, alone,
Feeling old.

Poor is a tired face.
Poor is thin.
Poor is standing outside
Looking in.

Their feet, planted into tar,
drew them down,
back to the core of birth,
and all they are
is found in earth,
recovered, bone by bone,
rising again, like stone
skeletons, naked, white,
to live again, staring,
head holes glaring,
towering, proud, tall,
in some museum hall.

The storm is on.
The rumbling thunder is on again
And the hammers flash and
Pound on the mountains
And the wheels of Thor's chariot
Come tumbling down the sky.

If only I
Had iron gloves and a magic belt
I could turn it all off—
Just like that!

Abstract Picture: At the Museum

It is a slice of moon, they cry,
A slice of slivered moon in a green sky

(Perhaps); it is a melon in the grass.
Its seeds spill slowly; it will pass

Into a flower, blooming wild and white
Against the darkness of a summer night's

Madness. (Perhaps); it is a tired stranger's face
In woods, in waves, in still another place

Deep within; (perhaps); it is a fish, a bird, a tree,
Or all the pictures you would make it be.

Just look at this ocean I made
With waves and everything
Swishing up and down
Splashing over me,
With small islands (my knees)
Sticking up, and then sinking
Down, down.

My ocean bubbles with white foam
Of hundreds of soapsuds
Swirling all around,
And a soap boat
Sailing around the big island
(Which is me) and then sinking
Down, down.

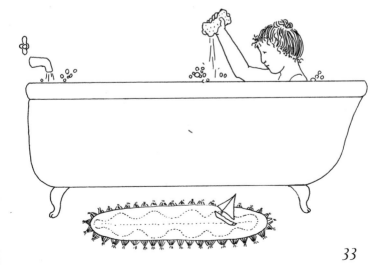

Inside the fortune cooky
I found a slip of paper.

You will be prosperous and wise, it said.
And all good fortune will come to you.

> Which got me to thinking
> about a stereo and a Porsche and all
> the records in the stores and
> a Nikon and a ten-speed bicycle
> and a big house and a swimming pool
> and tennis courts, and stuff like that.

Oh, the prosperous part is fine,
The good fortune.
But how does *wise* grab you?

Nobody knows what's there but me,
   knows where I keep my silver key
   and my baseball cards
   and my water gun
   and my wind-up car that doesn't run,
   and a stone I found with a hole clear through
   and a blue-jay feather that's *mostly* blue,
   and a note that I wrote to the guy next door
   and never gave him—and lots, lots more
   of important things that I'll never show
   to anyone, *anyone* else I know.

Whoever's the new baby around here
  has it o.k.
Just crying and eating and sleeping all day.
No schoolwork.
No chores.
No trash to empty.
No slamming doors.
No nothing to do but lie around and play.

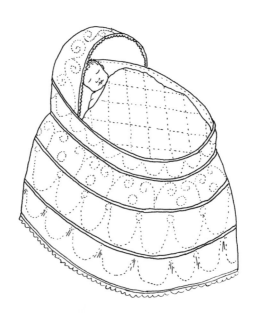

Now that's what I call a real mountain.
Solid. Chock-full of big hard rocks.
Some trees stick out with bare roots
Gnarled around. Some green stuff creeps
Along. Lots of places for snakes to hide.
Maybe a couple of squirrels. A rabbit dashes off.
And you can climb and climb and climb
And never get to the top.

A friend sent me some seeds.
 Snow-on-the-mountain,
 Euphorbia.
 "Triple-tested seeds,
 "An interesting foliage plant with deeply veined
  leaves."

It says the leaves will be silvery white,
Good for borders.

And I'm shaking the packet.
It sounds *cristly*.

I'm wondering how they would look.
 Snow-on-the-mountain,
 Euphorbia.
 How they will be,
 These Mandeville seeds my friends sent to me.

(Lord, find me a garden to grow my seeds,
A garden with a border,
A mountain, some snow,
And now and again, a dandelion.)

I think I know just how the notes should sound,
And yet there's always something in the way
The violins, the horns and woodwinds play
That makes me understand that I have found

A kind of hearing that is strange and new,
A music I have never heard before,
And so I listen   listen more,
Asking what it is that Mozart knew

That I must find myself, and hear, although
The next time that I play it, some new phrase
Will whirl within my head for days and days
And come to be a part of all I know.

Once, dwarfs ran in cavernous mountains
from an ugly dragon. Hammer, hammer, chipping
hammer, hammer, and a hobbit came with a ring
in his hand.

The dragon is running. He is running.
His gold is lost to Bilbo Baggins.

So I take my coin from my hand,
Drop it into the turnstile
And I go.